VOCABULARY THROUGH IMAGERY

For All Ages

Volume 2

ANAISHA KERING

ZORBA BOOKS

Published by Zorba Books, February 2023
Website: www.zorbabooks.com
Email: info@zorbabooks.com
Author Name: ANAISHA KERING
Copyright ©: ANAISHA KERING

Title: VOCABULARY THROUGH IMAGERY

Printbook ISBN: 978-93-95217-42-2
Ebook ISBN: 978-93-95217-43-9

Zorba Books Pvt. Ltd. (opc)
Sushant Arcade,
Next to Courtyard Marriot,
Sushant Lok 1, Gurgaon – 122009, India

Printed in India

Anaisha Anish Kering has set a Record in 'India Book of Records' in 2021 at the age of 5.

Anaisha Anish Kering has set a Record in 'International Book Of Records' in 2022 at the age of 6.

'World Book of Records' has conferred the title of 'Youngest Author' on Anaisha Anish Kering in 2022.

About the Author

Anaisha Kering is a standard 2 student of St. Mary's school, Pune Maharashtra.

Anaisha Anish Kering has set INTERNATIONAL RECORDS by writing and publishing 2 books at the age of 6.

She has been bestowed with "Global titles" as below:

1. *YOUNGEST AUTHOR*
    by the
    WORLD BOOK OF RECORDS(LONDON)
2. *YOUNGEST WORDSMITH*
    by the
    INTERNATIONAL BOOK OF RECORDS

https://internationalbookofrecords.com/records/youngest-wordsmith-to-write-and-publish-maximum-books

https://www.youtube.com/watch?v=JDF06oYO7p0

Anaisha Anish Kering has written two books:

1. Vocabulary through Imagery
2. Bucketful of Beatitudes

The same have been published and are available on Amazon, Kindle, Flipkart and Goodreads, in India and on Amazon globally.

About the Author

The hardcopies of the books are currently available in Oxford bookstores in Delhi and Mumbai and Crossword bookstore in Pune.

She has set a record in "INDIA BOOK OF RECORDS" for being the youngest to pronounce and spell the 10 longest English words within 3 minutes at the age of 6. She won a Merit award in a National Level Rubik Cube Championship in Mumbai at the age of 4.5 years. She is a child prodigy with exemplary brain and memory. She has won many awards for her story narration, poetry and creative art skills. She has been interviewed by many newspapers and has received digital media coverage pan India.

She is recognized as "India's Young Wonder" by Intelligence plus and News shuttle.

1. Anaisha has set a record in "INDIA BOOK OF RECORDS" for pronouncing and spelling the 10 longest English words within 3 minutes at the age of 6 yrs. She is the Youngest in India to achieve this feat.

   https://www.youtube.com/watch?v=qHlm6bzVxF0

This achievement has received digital media coverage pan India.

Also, recently this achievement has been telecasted on 2 national TV channels viz. Sudarshan TV and Sadhana channel.

Also, the same has been featured on various online portals.

https://influencerstoday.blogspot.com/2021/07/anaisha-kering-creates-record-for.html?m=1

https://risingindiastar.blogspot.com/2021/07/reciting-longest-words-is-childs-play.html?m=1

2. She won a Merit award (trophy) in a National Level Rubik Cube Championship held in Mumbai, at the age of 4.5 years.

3. She has been interviewed by NEWSSHUTTLE (newspaper for kids) for memorizing and recalling a deck of cards and for solving the Rubik's cube without looking.

https://www.youtube.com/watch?v=c5i3oRFVE5o

4. She has been awarded 'The Child Prodigy Award 2021' for being among the 'Top 100 Prodigies of the World'.

5. Bharat Olympiad foundation has recognized her talent and has awarded her for the same.

6. She won the 1st prize in Tell-Ur-Tale Challenge organized by WizkidsCarnival at the age of 5. Her story has been published in their e-magazine.

7. Along with her cubing (3 cubes) and Storytelling skills, she was recognized as "INDIA'S YOUNG WONDER" by Intelligence Plus and the same was featured in their online parenting summit.

8. She won the 3rd prize for composing and narrating a beautiful poem in the "Rhyme your thoughts" challenge organized by WizkidsCarnival.

9. She has earned the "Rising Artist title award" in all India National level art contest organized by Art Chitrakala.

10. Have won medals in sports day in Prim Rose and St. Mary's school.

11. She has won an Honorable Mention award as a Master Orator in an Elocution competition.
12. She has won 'The most innovative Salad' award in a salad making competition organized by Toss it.
13. She has won a 'Spectacular Performer' award, from 'Knack Hunt' for all her skills and achievements.
14. She solves a 6by6 Sudoku puzzle in less than 2 minutes.

Acknowledgement

Expressing my gratitude and being grateful for things and people gives me immense happiness.

I am most grateful to my amazing Grandparents (My Aaji-Aajoba and my Dada-Dadi) for teaching me valuable life lessons, morals and to shape me into the person I am today.

I am thankful to my entire family for all their love, influence, encouragement and blessings.

I would like to thank all my friends and well wishers who constantly keep motivating and inspiring me to achieve my goals.

I would also like to thank all my readers.

I acknowledge and thank the editors and the entire Zorba Publishers team, without whom, my work would not have reached you.

I am eternally grateful to my treasures...My Mom and Dad, who have inculcated ethics, values, integrity and gratitude in me. They have always stimulated me to fly high and have turned my dream into reality.

Thank you God. Thank you Universe.

Truly grateful!

For One and All....

The "Vocabulary through Imagery" (word meaning) book is not restricted to any specific age group. Kids from age 5 to adults can refer the book to understand the technique of storing the words and their meanings in their long-term memory.

DOES THIS HAPPEN TO YOU??

Whenever we encounter an unfamiliar word in English, we refer a dictionary to know its meaning and mug it up. If we come across the same word after a few days, then mostly many of us cannot recollect the meaning. The reason is the word and its meaning gets deleted from our short term memory.

To store information in the long term memory, the Imaginative Instinct Replacement and Association (IIRA) technique (explained in this book) is strongly recommended.

Foreword

Language forms the core of learning which begins with alphabets and later takes the shape of words.

Vocabulary/ Lexicon:

- A catalyst to upgrade your linguistic skills.
- Enhances your word Power.
- Improves communication.
- Gets a grip on the language.

WHAT IS MEMORY?

MEMORY: 3 R's

1. Record
2. Retain
3. Recall

TYPES OF MEMORY:

1. SHORT TERM MEMORY: Lasts for a few seconds to few minutes.
2. MEDIUM TERM MEMORY: Lasts for few days to few weeks and eventually fades as time passes.
3. LONG TERM MEMORY: Lasts for months to years.

There is nothing like a good memory or bad memory. In fact there is trained memory and untrained memory.

With techniques, training and efforts, it is possible to convert short term and medium term memory into a long term memory.

Creativity and Imagination play a vital role in memorization. They are the most important ingredients for better assimilation, storage and recall.

With creativity, you can make your information unique. And as a matter of fact, unique information makes us curious and attracts our attention. And such unique information is easily remembered by our minds for a longer time than the common routine information.

"A PICTURE IS WORTH A THOUSAND WORDS".

<u>IMAGINATION:</u> Make it a habit to form a picture and visualize it, corresponding to the words or information.

<u>ASSOCIATION:</u> One of the key to good memorization. Associate new information with old information or the information you already know. The old information is always a bridge to reach to the new information. This bridge makes the retention and recall faster and easier.

A SCIENTIFIC TEHNIQUE

To store information in the long term memory, the Imaginative Instinct Replacement and Association (IIRA) technique is strongly recommended.

<u>Instinct:</u> First known word/words that come to your mind when you see or hear the unknown word. (Similar sounding, Rhyming, Small words put together to form that big word)

<u>Imagination, Replacement and Association:</u> Replace the unknown word with the instinct (known) word and Associate and Visualize the Instinct (known) word and the meaning of the word together.

The known word works like a bridge to reach to the meaning of the unknown word effortlessly.

This technique will make it easy for you to convert words in your short term memory into long term memory permanently.

If you memorize even 5 words everyday in this manner, then in a few months, you will create a vast vocabulary in your mind, helping you to communicate in English impressively.

VOCABULARY THROUGH IMAGERY
For All Ages

Volume 2

1. Convivial: Friendly, Lively, Enjoyable

Imaginative Instinct Replacement:

Convivial ---- Corn + Vivo (phone)

Association: Associate corn+Vivo to the meaning of the word Convivial.

Association Example:

A Corn and Vivo phone went to watch a cricket match together. The atmosphere over there was very friendly and lively.

STRIKE OUT!
(Give it a try…)

What is your?

<u>Imaginative Instinct Replacement:</u>

<u>Association Example:</u>

----

2. Xenodochial: Friendly to Strangers or Guests

<u>Imaginative Instinct Replacement:</u>

Xenodochial ---- Zen + Dough + Koyal

<u>Association:</u> Associate Zen+dough+koyal to the meaning of the word xenodochial.

<u>Association Example:</u>

When zen, dough (Playdoh) and koyal meet together for their secret missions, they are very friendly to all the strangers and guests.

STRIKE OUT!
(Give it a try...)

What is your?

Imaginative Instinct Replacement:

Association Example:

----

3. Fastidious: Very Attentive to, Concerned about Accuracy

<u>Imaginative Instinct Replacement:</u>

Fastidious ---- Fast + Tedious

Association: Associate Fast+Tedious to the meaning of the word fastidious.

<u>Association Example:</u>

Anaisha and her pals went for a trek. Initially they were fast and very attentive towards the climb. But later, the trek became very tedious (tiring).

STRIKE OUT!
(Give it a try…)

What is your?

<u>Imaginative Instinct Replacement:</u>

Association Example:

----

4. Nifty: Skillful, Attractive

<u>Imaginative Instinct Replacement:</u>

Nifty --- Ninety

Association: Associate Ninety to the meaning of the word Nifty.

<u>Association Example:</u>

The old lady was ninety (90 years). But still she was very skillful and attractive.

STRIKE OUT!
(Give it a try…)

What is your?

<u>Imaginative Instinct Replacement:</u>

<u>**Association Example:**</u>

----

5. Trailblazing: Innovative

<u>Imaginative Instinct Replacement:</u>

Trailblazing ---- Train + Gazing

Association: Associate Train+gazing to the meaning of the word trailblazing.

Association Example:

One day, Anaisha was gazing at a train. While gazing at the train, she got an innovative idea that she can think of making a flying train.

STRIKE OUT!
(Give it a try…)

What is your?

Imaginative Instinct Replacement:

Association Example:

----

6. Gallant: Brave, Heroic

<u>Imaginative Instinct Replacement:</u>

Gallant --- Gal + Land

Association: Associate Gal + Land to the meaning of the word gallant.

<u>Association Example:</u>

A gal was flying a fighter jet. It ran out of fuel. The gal was very brave to land the jet in an open space in the jungle.

STRIKE OUT!
(Give it a try…)

What is your?

<u>Imaginative Instinct Replacement:</u>

<u>Association Example:</u>

----

7. Euphoric: Feeling of Intense Excitement and Happiness

Imaginative Instinct Replacement:

Euphoric --- You + 4 + Rick

Association: Associate you + 4 + Rick to the meaning of the word euphoric.

Association Example:

When I (Anaisha) see You (Rhea) sitting in 4 Ricks one by one, I get a feeling of intense excitement and happiness.

STRIKE OUT!
(Give it a try…)

What is your?

<u>Imaginative Instinct Replacement:</u>

<u>**Association Example:**</u>

----

8. Perky: Cheerful and Lively

<u>Imaginative Instinct Replacement:</u>

Perky ---- Perk + Key

Association: Associate Perk + Key to the meaning of the word perky.

<u>Association Example:</u>

One day, Anaisha was very sad. So she ate a Perk chocolate. A golden key came out of the chocolate and started dancing and singing. This made Anaisha feel very cheerful and lively.

STRIKE OUT!
(Give it a try...)

What is your?

Imaginative Instinct Replacement:

Association Example:

----

9. Brawny: Physically Strong, Muscular

<u>Imaginative Instinct Replacement:</u>

Brawny ---- Brownie

Association: Associate Brownie to the meaning of the word brawny.

Association Example:

A chocolate brownie was placed under a huge cake. It was very strong and muscular to bear the weight of the entire 3 layered cake.

STRIKE OUT!
(Give it a try…)

What is your?

<u>Imaginative Instinct Replacement:</u>

<u>Association Example:</u>

----

10. Snazzy: Stylish and Attractive

<u>Imaginative Instinct Replacement:</u>

Snazzy ---- Sneezy

Association: Associate sneezy to the meaning of the word snazzy.

<u>Association Example:</u>

When Anaisha was small, she used to sneeze in a very stylish and attractive manner. After sneezing, she used to say sneezy sneezy.

STRIKE OUT!
(Give it a try…)

What is your?

<u>Imaginative Instinct Replacement:</u>

<u>Association Example:</u>

----

11. Prudent: Wise or Judicious, Careful

<u>Imaginative Instinct Replacement:</u>

Prudent ---- Pru + dent

Association: Associate Pru + dent to the meaning of the word prudent.

<u>Association Example:</u>

Pru (a girl in Spirit) bumped into a tree, while driving the car. The car got a dent. Pru was very wise and careful to repair the dent, so that no one sees it.

STRIKE OUT!
(Give it a try…)

What is your?

Imaginative Instinct Replacement:

Association Example:

----

12. Scrupulous: Careful, Very Concerned to Avoid Doing Wrong

<u>Imaginative Instinct Replacement:</u>

Scrupulous --- Screw + Puke + Lassi

Association: Associate Screw+Puke+Lassi to the meaning of the word scrupulous

<u>Association Example:</u>

Anaisha's friend Shanaya drank a glass of lassi that had a screw in it, so she puked. While puking, she was being very careful that the screw does not hurt her.

STRIKE OUT!
(Give it a try…)

What is your?

<u>Imaginative Instinct Replacement:</u>

<u>**Association Example:**</u>

----

13. Didactic: Designed or Intended to Teach

Imaginative Instinct Replacement:

Didactic --- Duck + Tactic

Association: Associate Duck + Tactic to the meaning of the word didactic.

Association Example:

The duck in the lake had some good tactics to escape from its enemies. And it intended to teach the tactics to her ducklings.

STRIKE OUT!
(Give it a try...)

What is your?

<u>Imaginative Instinct Replacement:</u>

<u>**Association Example:**</u>

----

14. Iridescent: Lustrous or Colorful in Appearance

<u>Imaginative Instinct Replacement:</u>

Iridescent --- Ira + Decent

Association: Associate Ira + Decent to the meaning of the word Iridescent.

<u>Association Example:</u>

Anaisha's friend Ira calls herself decent. But she is always dressed in lustrous and colorful clothes.

STRIKE OUT!
(Give it a try…)

What is your?

<u>Imaginative Instinct Replacement:</u>

<u>Association Example:</u>

----

15. Demure: Modest and Shy, Reserved (Used for a Women)

<u>Imaginative Instinct Replacement:</u>

Demure ---- Dim + Your

Association: Associate Dim + Your to the meaning of the word demure.

<u>Association Example:</u>

Anaisha went to Mahi's house for a dance party. She was very shy and reserved to dance in front of everyone. So Anaisha told her "Dim your light", so that no one sees you dancing.

STRIKE OUT!
(Give it a try…)

What is your?

<u>Imaginative Instinct Replacement:</u>

<u>Association Example:</u>

----

16. Vivacious: Full of Energy and Enthusiasm

<u>Imaginative Instinct Replacement:</u>

Vivacious ---- Wow + Wave + Shreyas (Iyer)

Association: Associate Wow+wave+Shreyas to the meaning of the word vivacious.

<u>Association Example:</u>

When Shreyas went to the beach, he said Wow! Looking at the waves and waved at them. This action of his was full of energy and enthusiasm.

STRIKE OUT!
(Give it a try…)

What is your?

<u>Imaginative Instinct Replacement:</u>

<u>Association Example:</u>

----

17. Stoic: A Person who can Endure Pain, without Showing their Feelings or without Complaining.

<u>Imaginative Instinct Replacement:</u>

Stoic ---- Stock

Association: Associate Stock to the meaning of the word Stoic.

Association Example:

Anaisha had to carry the entire stock of books from her home library to school every day. She bore the pain of carrying the big and heavy books and yet did not complain about it.

STRIKE OUT!
(Give it a try…)

What is your?

Imaginative Instinct Replacement:

Association Example:

----

18. Plucky: Courageous

<u>Imaginative Instinct Replacement:</u>

Plucky --- Pluck

Association: Associate Pluck to the meaning of the word Plucky.

<u>Association Example:</u>

Anaisha was very courageous to pluck flowers from a dense and scary forest.

STRIKE OUT!
(Give it a try...)

What is your?

Imaginative Instinct Replacement:

Association Example:

----

19. Effusive: Showing or Expressing Gratitude

<u>Imaginative Instinct Replacement:</u>

Effusive ---- A + Few + Zips

Association: Associate A + Few + Zips to the meaning of the word effusive.

Association Example:

One day Anaisha went to a mall. There she found a store that had decorative, colorful buttons, zips etc. She saw a few golden zips and decided to buy them. The zips expressed gratitude towards her for buying them.

STRIKE OUT!
(Give it a try...)

What is your?

<u>Imaginative Instinct Replacement:</u>

<u>Association Example:</u>

----

20. Urbane: Polite, Polished

<u>Imaginative Instinct Replacement:</u>

Urbane --- Urban (Urban Company UC)

Association: Associate Urban to the meaning of the word urbane.

<u>Association Example:</u>

The Urban Company people who come home for services are very polite and their behavior is quite polished.

STRIKE OUT!
(Give it a try…)

What is your?

<u>Imaginative Instinct Replacement:</u>

Association Example:

----

21. Jammy: Lucky

<u>Imaginative Instinct Replacement:</u>

Jammy --- Jam

Association: Associate jam to the meaning of the word jammy.

Association Example:

Anaisha was about to spread the jam on her toast. But she changed her mind. The jam said, 'Thank you, I am so lucky that you did not eat me up'.

STRIKE OUT!
(Give it a try…)

What is your?

<u>Imaginative Instinct Replacement:</u>

<u>Association Example:</u>

----

22. Hunky-Dory: Fine, Going Well

<u>Imaginative Instinct Replacement:</u>

Hunky-dory ---- Hunk (Handsome, attractive man) + Dory (Fish)

Association: Associate hunk + dory to the meaning of the word hunky-dory.

<u>Association Example:</u>

In Maldives, Anaisha saw a Dory(fish) and it was a handsome hunk. She tried to play with it and catch it. But still Dory pretended to be fine.

STRIKE OUT!
(Give it a try…)

What is your?

<u>Imaginative Instinct Replacement:</u>

<u>Association Example:</u>

----

23. Copacetic: In Excellent order, Going Well.

<u>Imaginative Instinct Replacement:</u>

Copacetic --- Cop (police) + set + tick

Association: Associate Cop+set+tick to the meaning of the word copacetic.

<u>Association Example:</u>

The cop was all set for his duty but realized that he was late. But still he put tick mark in the register to indicate that everything was going well and in excellent order.

STRIKE OUT!
(Give it a try…)

What is your?

<u>Imaginative Instinct Replacement:</u>

<u>Association Example:</u>

----

24. Bountiful: Abundant, Large in Quantity

<u>Imaginative Instinct Replacement:</u>

Bountiful --- Bounty (Dad's favorite chocolate) + Full

Association: Associate bounty + full to the meaning of the word bountiful.

<u>Association Example:</u>

A field was full of bounty chocolates. And the bounty chocolates were large in quantity that they covered the entire farm.

STRIKE OUT!
(Give it a try...)

What is your?

<u>Imaginative Instinct Replacement:</u>

<u>Association Example:</u>

----

25. Beguiling: Charming, Interesting, Enchanting

<u>Imaginative Instinct Replacement:</u>

Beguiling ---- Bee + Guy (Man) + link

Association: Associate bee+guy+link to the meaning of the word beguiling.

<u>Association Example:</u>

A bee and a guy (man) were joined together by a link. This structure (creature) looked very charming and interesting.

STRIKE OUT!
(Give it a try…)

What is your?

<u>Imaginative Instinct Replacement:</u>

<u>Association Example:</u>

----

26. Diligent: Done in a Careful and Detailed Way

<u>Imaginative Instinct Replacement:</u>

Diligent ---- Delhi + Gent(Men)

Association: Associate Delhi + gent to the meaning of the word diligent.

Association Example:

In Delhi, all the gents (men) do their work in a careful and detailed way.

STRIKE OUT!
(Give it a try...)

What is your?

<u>Imaginative Instinct Replacement:</u>

<u>Association Example:</u>

----

27. Ebullient: Cheerful and Full of Energy

<u>Imaginative Instinct Replacement:</u>

Ebullient --- A bullet

Association: Associate a bullet to the meaning of the word ebullient.

Association Example:

A bullet was very cheerful and full of energy; when it heard that it was going to go in the gun and be shot at the target.

STRIKE OUT!
(Give it a try...)

What is your?

<u>Imaginative Instinct Replacement:</u>

<u>Association Example:</u>

----

28. Gregarious: Friendly, Social

<u>Imaginative Instinct Replacement:</u>

Gregarious --- Gregory (Boys name)

Association: Associate Gregory to the meaning of the word gregarious.

<u>Association Example:</u>

A boy named Gregory came to my society. And he was very friendly and social with all my friends.

STRIKE OUT!
(Give it a try…)

What is your?

Imaginative Instinct Replacement:

Association Example:

----

29. Suave: Charming, Confident and Elegant (Used aor a Man)

<u>Imaginative Instinct Replacement:</u> Suave --- Wow

Association: Associate wow to the meaning of the word Suave.

<u>Association Example:</u>

One day a charming, confident and elegant man came to Anaisha's school. All the kids looked at him and said 'wow!' and ran towards him to take his autograph.

STRIKE OUT!
(Give it a try...)

What is your?

<u>Imaginative Instinct Replacement:</u>

<u>Association Example:</u>

----

30. Ambrosial: Having a Very Pleasant Taste or Smell

Imaginative Instinct Replacement:

Ambrosial --- (I) Am + Bro + Shield

Association: Associate Am + Bro + shield to the meaning of the word ambrosial.

Association Example:

I and my bro went to a restaurant with a shield, and ordered our food. The food had a very pleasant taste and smell.

STRIKE OUT!
(Give it a try...)

What is your?

<u>Imaginative Instinct Replacement:</u>

<u>Association Example:</u>

----

31. Benignant: Kind and Benevolent

<u>Imaginative Instinct Replacement:</u>

Benignant --- Ben (Ben10) + Grunt

Association: Associate Ben + grunt to the meaning of the word benignant.

<u>Association Example:</u>

Ben has a habit of grunting. The grunting gives him the power to be kind, helpful and benevolent to people.

STRIKE OUT!
(Give it a try...)

What is your?

<u>Imaginative Instinct Replacement:</u>

<u>**Association Example:**</u>

----

32. Refulgent: Shining Very Brightly, Radiant

<u>Imaginative Instinct Replacement:</u>

Refulgent --- Detergent

Association: Associate detergent to the meaning of the word refulgent.

<u>Association Example:</u>

When Anaisha opened a packet of detergent, golden rays came out of the packet and the detergent started shining bright.

STRIKE OUT!
(Give it a try...)

What is your?

Imaginative Instinct Replacement:

Association Example:

----

33. Saccharine: Extremely Sweet

<u>Imaginative Instinct Replacement:</u>

Saccharine --- Sac + marine

Association: Associate sac + marine to the meaning of the word saccharine.

<u>Association Example:</u>

A mermaid was carrying a sac of chocolates to distribute it among the animals. After eating the chocolates, the animals told her that the chocolates were extremely sweet and sugary.

STRIKE OUT!
(Give it a try...)

What is your?

Imaginative Instinct Replacement:

Association Example:

----

34. Adept: Very Skilled, Proficient at Something

<u>Imaginative Instinct Replacement:</u>

Adept --- A depth

Association: Associate a depth to the meaning of the word adept.

Association Example:

In the jungle, there was a well and it had a great depth. The well was very skilled to tilt itself, so that the animals could drink water easily.

STRIKE OUT!
(Give it a try...)

What is your?

<u>Imaginative Instinct Replacement:</u>

<u>Association Example:</u>

----

35. Splendiferous: Splendid, Very Beautiful

<u>Imaginative Instinct Replacement:</u>

Splendiferous --- Splendid + Fanus (Jackfruit)

Association: Associate splendid + fanus to the meaning of the word splendiferous.

<u>Association Example:</u>

One day Anaisha saw a square fanus in Nandanvan farmhouse. She touched it and it turned into a beautiful and splendid lilac fanus.

STRIKE OUT!
(Give it a try...)

What is your?

Imaginative Instinct Replacement:

Association Example:

----

36. Placid: Calm, Peaceful, Easy Going

<u>Imaginative Instinct Replacement:</u>

Placid --- Plastic

Association: Associate plastic to the meaning of the word placid.

Association Example:

The President banned plastic in the country. So people started throwing plastic in the dustbin. The plastic liked being in the dustbin, and hence it was very calm and peaceful.

STRIKE OUT!
(Give it a try...)

What is your?

Imaginative Instinct Replacement:

Association Example:

----

37. Stupendous: Extremely Impressive

<u>Imaginative Instinct Replacement:</u>

Stupendous ---- Stew + Pen + Dust

Association: Associate stew + pen + dust to the meaning of the word stupendous.

Association Example:

Anaisha's teacher, Aroza miss asked the students to cook a dish and get it to school. Anaisha cooked a dish with stew, pen and dust and took it to school. Her teacher said that this is extremely impressive because it was in her favorite color yellow.

STRIKE OUT!
(Give it a try…)

What is your?

<u>Imaginative Instinct Replacement:</u>

<u>Association Example:</u>

----

38. Poised: Composed, Marked by Balance

<u>Imaginative Instinct Replacement:</u>

Poised --- Paused

Association: Associate paused to the meaning of the word poised.

<u>Association Example:</u>

One day Anaisha was playing a game on the ipad. And she paused the game every now and then. The game did not get angry; instead it was calm and composed.

STRIKE OUT!
(Give it a try...)

What is your?

<u>Imaginative Instinct Replacement:</u>

<u>Association Example:</u>

----

39. Debonair: Confident, Stylish and Charming (Typically used for a Man)

<u>Imaginative Instinct Replacement:</u>

Debonair --- Deaf + air

Association: Associate deaf + air to the meaning of the word debonair.

Association Example:

Anaisha had a magical power that she could see, talk and play with air. Though the air was deaf, it was confident, stylish and charming while playing with Anaisha.

STRIKE OUT!
(Give it a try...)

What is your?

<u>Imaginative Instinct Replacement:</u>

<u>**Association Example:**</u>

----

40. Thrifty: Using Money and Other Resources Carefully and Not Wastefully

<u>Imaginative Instinct Replacement:</u>

Thrifty ---- Thirsty

Association: Associate thirsty to the meaning of the word thrifty.

Association Example:

One day, Anaisha was very thirsty. So she drank an entire jug of water. At the bottom of the jug, she found lots of money. She decided to use this money very carefully and not wastefully.

STRIKE OUT!
(Give it a try…)

What is your?

<u>Imaginative Instinct Replacement:</u>

<u>**Association Example:**</u>

----

41. Gullible: Innocent, Easily Persuaded to believe Something

<u>Imaginative Instinct Replacement:</u>

Gullible --- Gulp + able

Association: Associate gulp + able to the meaning of the word gullible.

Association Example:

Anaisha told her little brother Shaurya, that we can gulp the word 'able'. He was so innocent that he believed her very easily.

STRIKE OUT!
(Give it a try...)

What is your?

<u>Imaginative Instinct Replacement:</u>

<u>**Association Example:**</u>

----

42. Resolute: Determined, Being Admirably Purposeful

Imaginative Instinct Replacement:

Resolute --- Race + loot (robbery)

Association: Associate race + loot to the meaning of the word resolute.

Association Example:

The robbers wanted to loot Anaisha's books. They ran a race and were determined to win it.

STRIKE OUT!
(Give it a try...)

What is your?

<u>Imaginative Instinct Replacement:</u>

<u>**Association Example:**</u>

----

43. Valiant: Possessing or Showing Courage or Bravery

<u>Imaginative Instinct Replacement:</u>

Valiant ---- Valley + Ant

Association: Associate valley + ant to the meaning of the word valiant.

Association Example:

The ant fell in the big valley of Mt. Everest. But it showed a lot of courage and bravery to climb the valley and come up.

STRIKE OUT!
(Give it a try...)

What is your?

<u>Imaginative Instinct Replacement:</u>

<u>Association Example:</u>

----

44. Palpable: Able to be Touched or Felt

<u>Imaginative Instinct Replacement:</u>

Palpable --- pal + pebble

Association: Associate pal + pebble to the meaning of the word palpable.

<u>Association Example:</u>

Anaisha and her friends went for a hike. And along the stream, they saw multicolored pebbles, which they could actually touch and feel.

STRIKE OUT!
(Give it a try...)

What is your?

<u>Imaginative Instinct Replacement:</u>

<u>**Association Example:**</u>

----

45. Maelstrom: A Powerful Whirlpool in a Sea or a River

<u>Imaginative Instinct Replacement:</u>

Maelstrom --- Mail + Storm

Association: Associate mail + storm to the meaning of the word maelstrom.

<u>Association Example:</u>

Anaisha was on the beach. A postman got her a mail. When she opened the mail, a big storm came and it caused a powerful whirlpool in the sea.

STRIKE OUT!
(Give it a try…)

What is your?

<u>Imaginative Instinct Replacement:</u>

<u>Association Example:</u>

----

46. Mellifluous: Pleasingly Smooth and Musical to Hear

<u>Imaginative Instinct Replacement:</u>

Mellifluous --- Mili + flew + us

Association: Associate Mili + flew + us to the meaning of the word mellifluous.

<u>Association Example:</u>

Mili flew us (Anaisha and her friends) around the world on a magical carpet and sang songs for us in her soft and musical voice.

STRIKE OUT!
(Give it a try…)

What is your?

Imaginative Instinct Replacement:

Association Example:

----

47. Gingerly: In a Careful or Cautious Manner

<u>Imaginative Instinct Replacement:</u>

Gingerly --- ginger

Association: Associate ginger to the meaning of the word gingerly.

<u>Association Example:</u>

The ginger was running in a careful and cautious manner, so that the old lady does not catch and grate it to put it in her tea.

STRIKE OUT!
(Give it a try...)

What is your?

Imaginative Instinct Replacement:

Association Example:

----

48. Adonis: A Young Man Who Looks Very Handsome

<u>Imaginative Instinct Replacement:</u>

Adonis --- a doughnut

Association: Associate a doughnut to the meaning of the word Adonis.

<u>Association Example:</u>

One night a handsome young man was walking on a street. He stepped on a chocolate gems doughnut and got trapped in the doughnut hole forever.

STRIKE OUT!
(Give it a try...)

What is your?

<u>Imaginative Instinct Replacement:</u>

<u>Association Example:</u>

----

49. Gourmet: A Person Who Has Good Taste in Food

<u>Imaginative Instinct Replacement:</u>

Gourmet --- Goa + May

Association: Associate Goa + May to the meaning of the word gourmet.

<u>Association Example:</u>

Anaisha went to Goa in May. Over there she met many tourists who had good taste in food. And they all made many waffles and Nutella pancakes for Anaisha.

STRIKE OUT!
(Give it a try…)

What is your?

<u>Imaginative Instinct Replacement:</u>

<u>**Association Example:**</u>

----

50. Herculean: Requiring Great Strength or Effort

<u>Imaginative Instinct Replacement:</u>

Herculean --- Her + Q + Lion

Association: Associate her + Q + lion to the meaning of the word herculean.

<u>Association Example:</u>

There was a lioness. Her name was 'Q' and her house was in Pune city. So she required great strength ad effort to hunt and find her prey in the city.

STRIKE OUT!
(Give it a try…)

What is your?

<u>Imaginative Instinct Replacement:</u>

<u>**Association Example:**</u>

----

51. Erudite: Having or Showing Great Knowledge or Learning

<u>Imaginative Instinct Replacement:</u>

Erudite --- A + Roo(k) + Diet

Association: Associate A + Roo(k) + Diet to the meaning of the word erudite.

Association Example:

The gym instructor in Anaisha's society had a great knowledge about foods and diets. So he would stop people (A + Roo(k)) and share his diets with them.

STRIKE OUT!
(Give it a try…)

What is your?

<u>Imaginative Instinct Replacement:</u>

<u>**Association Example:**</u>